I0468745

Swear Word Coloring Book

SwearWord Adult Coloring Book

Stress-Free Patterns

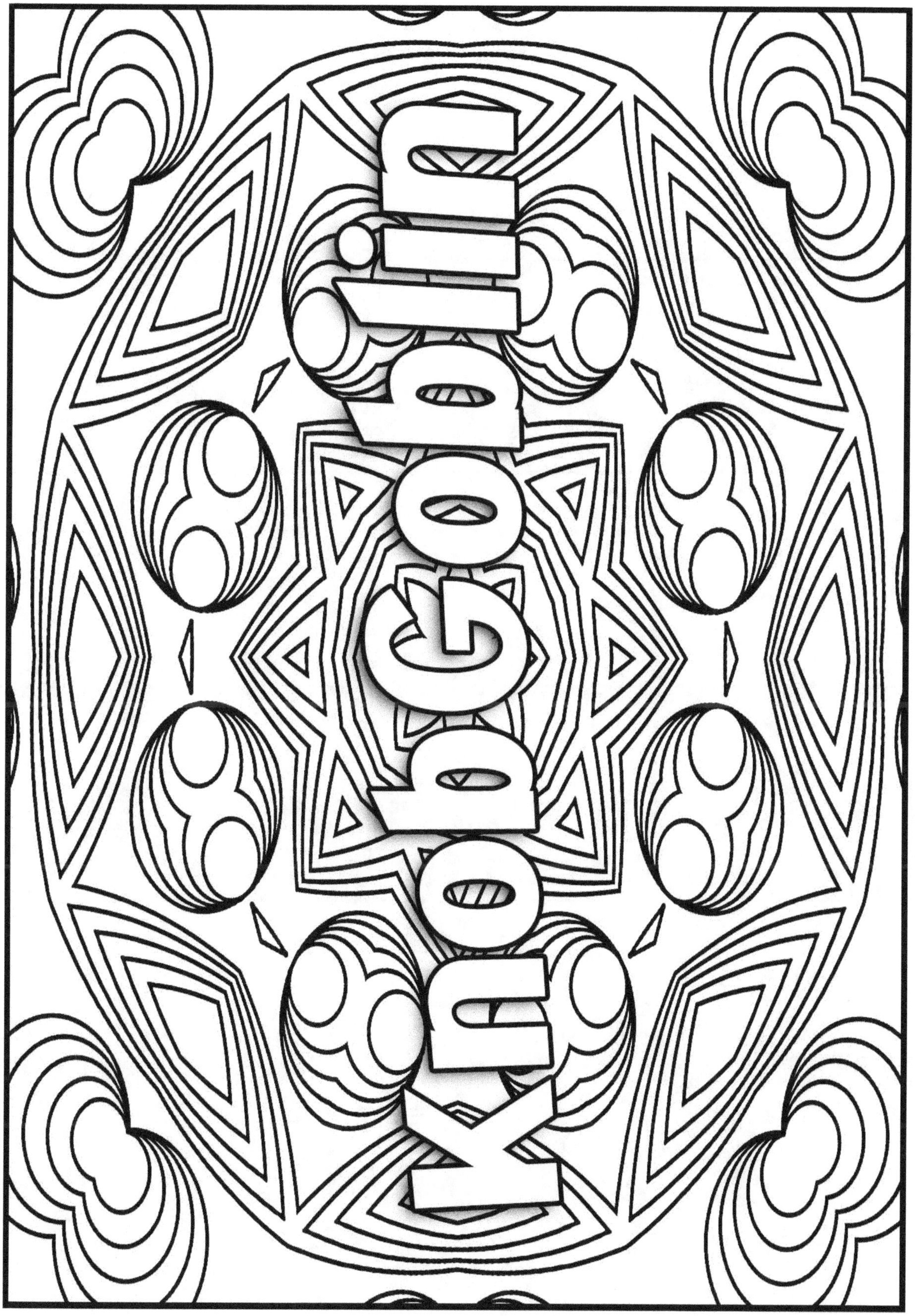
knobGoblin

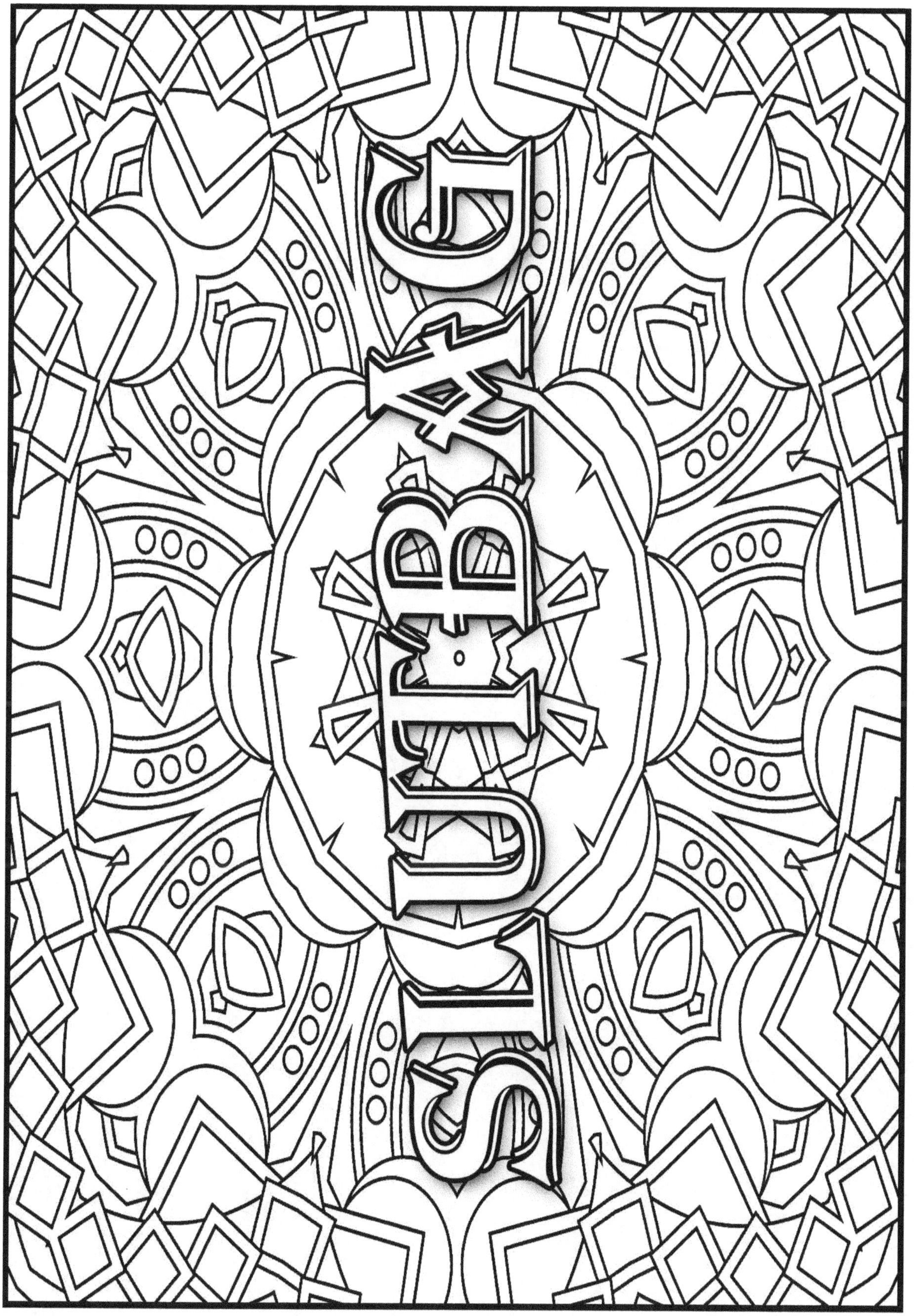
SHITBAG

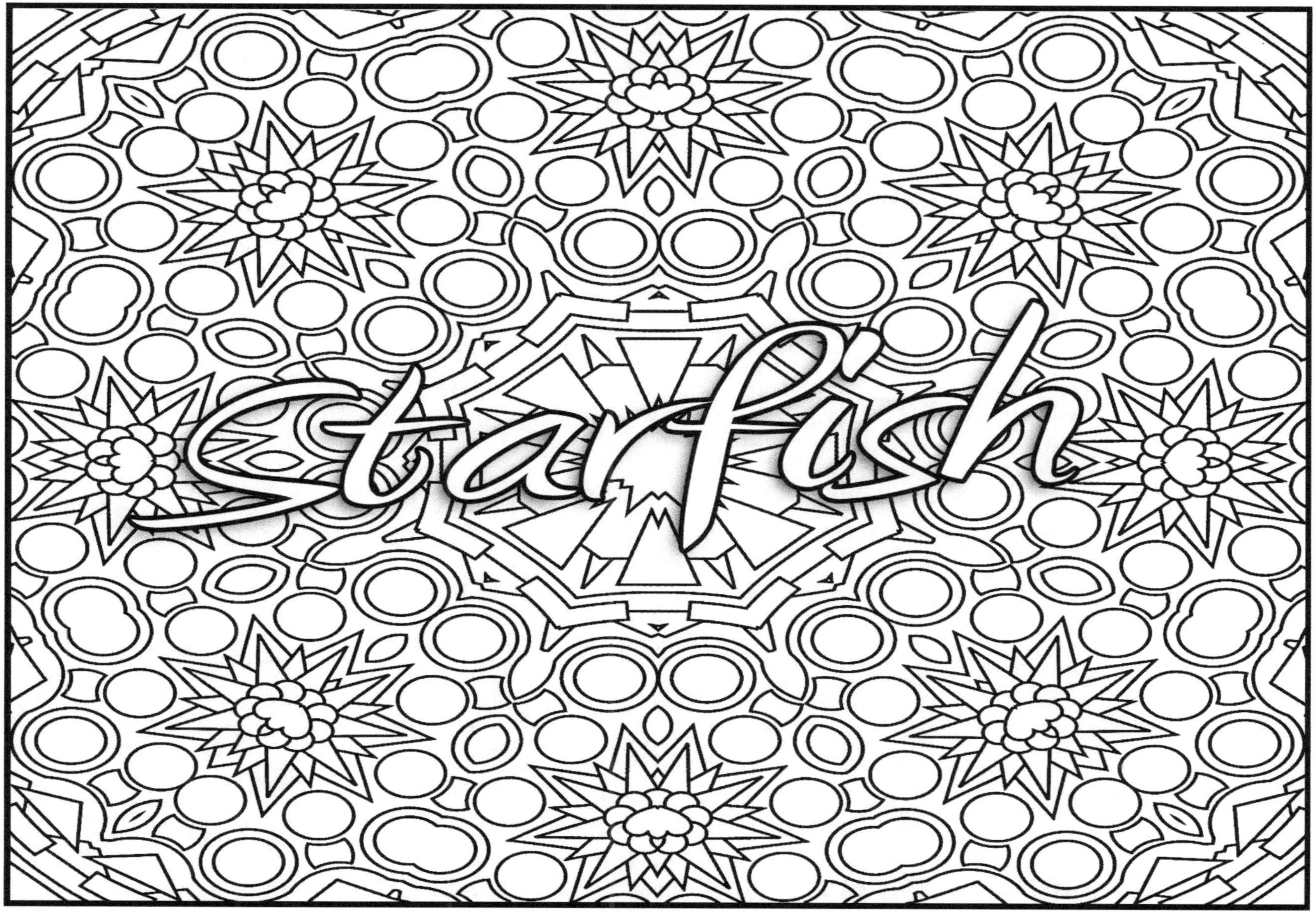
Starfish

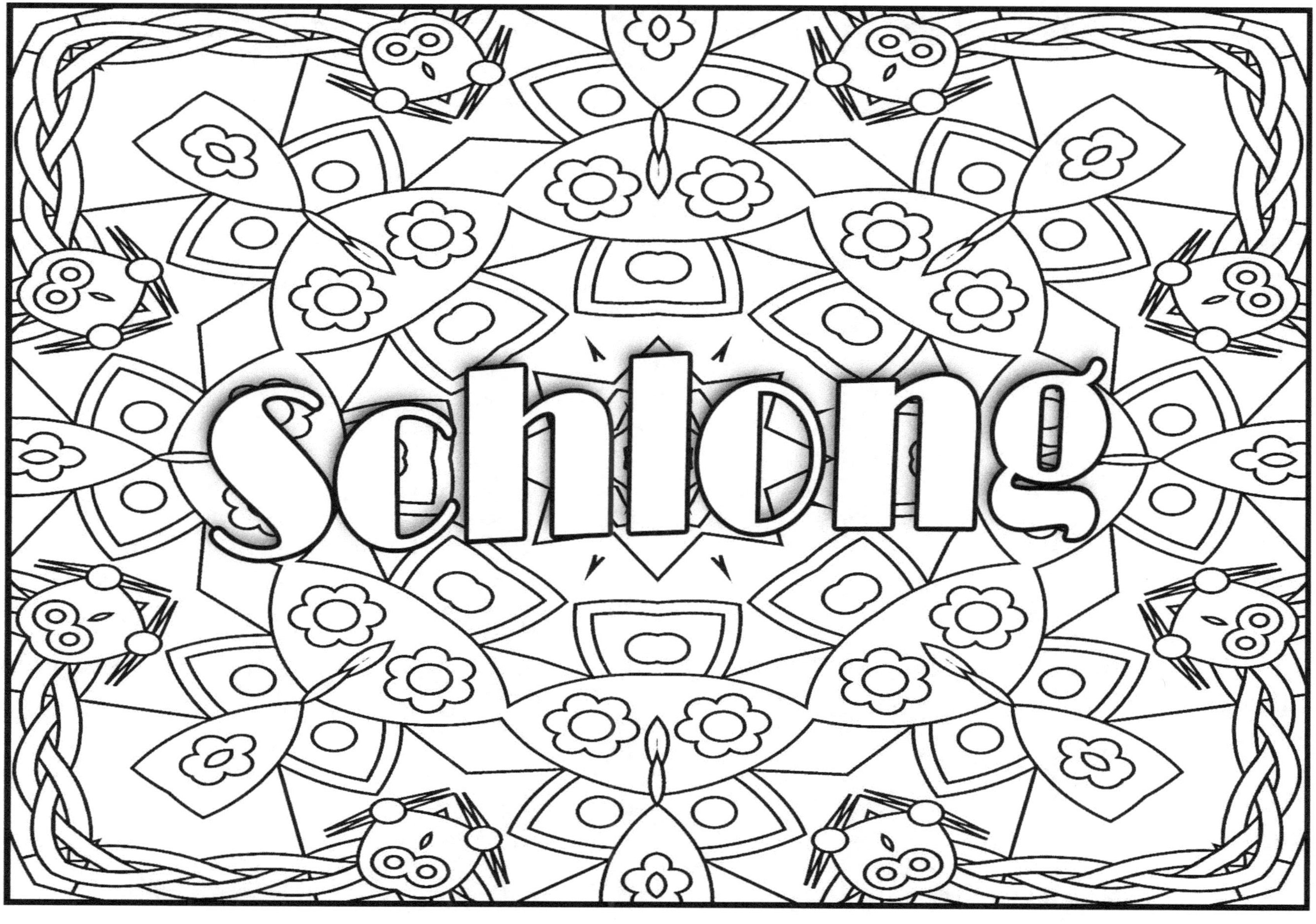
Schlong

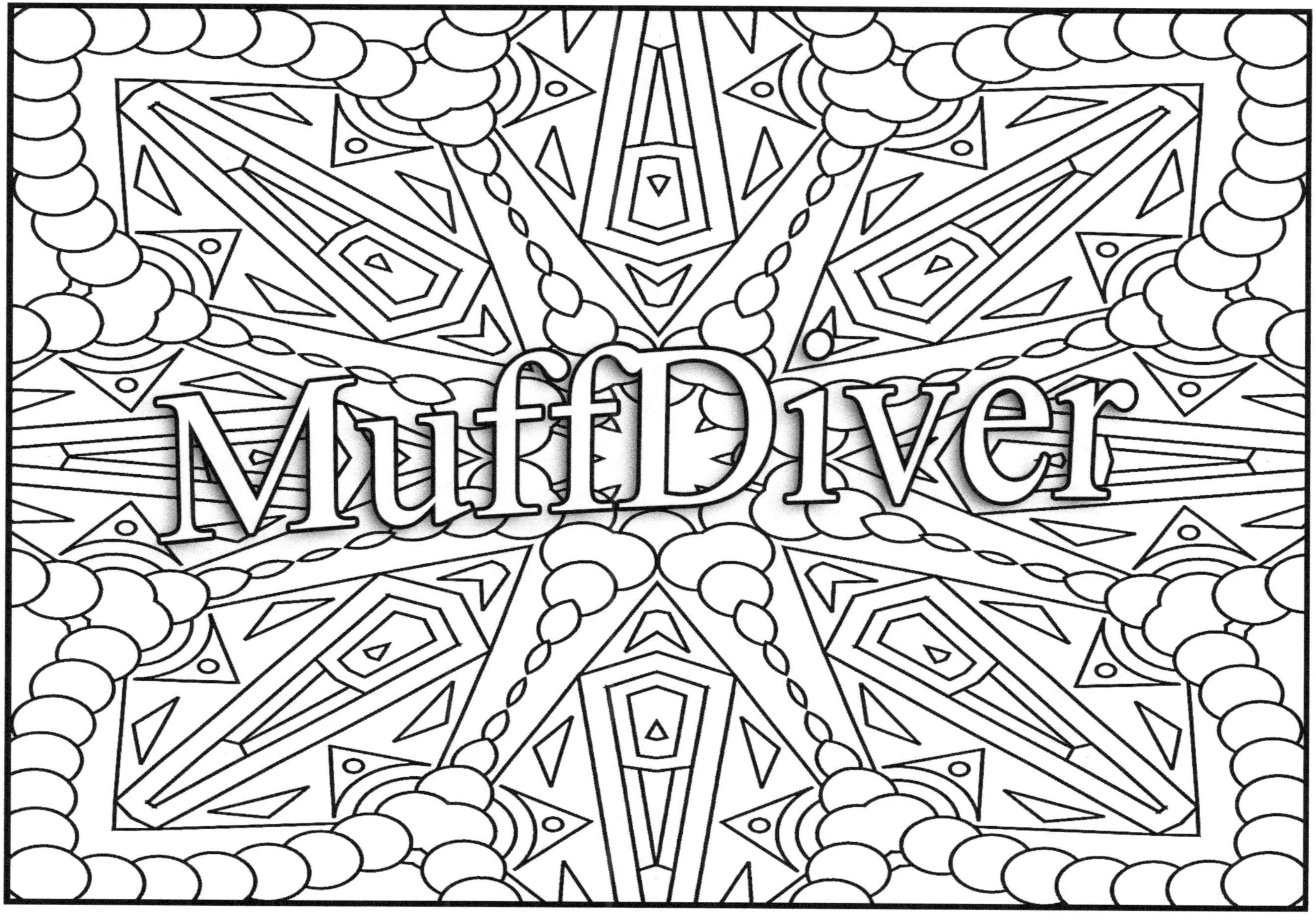
MuffDiver

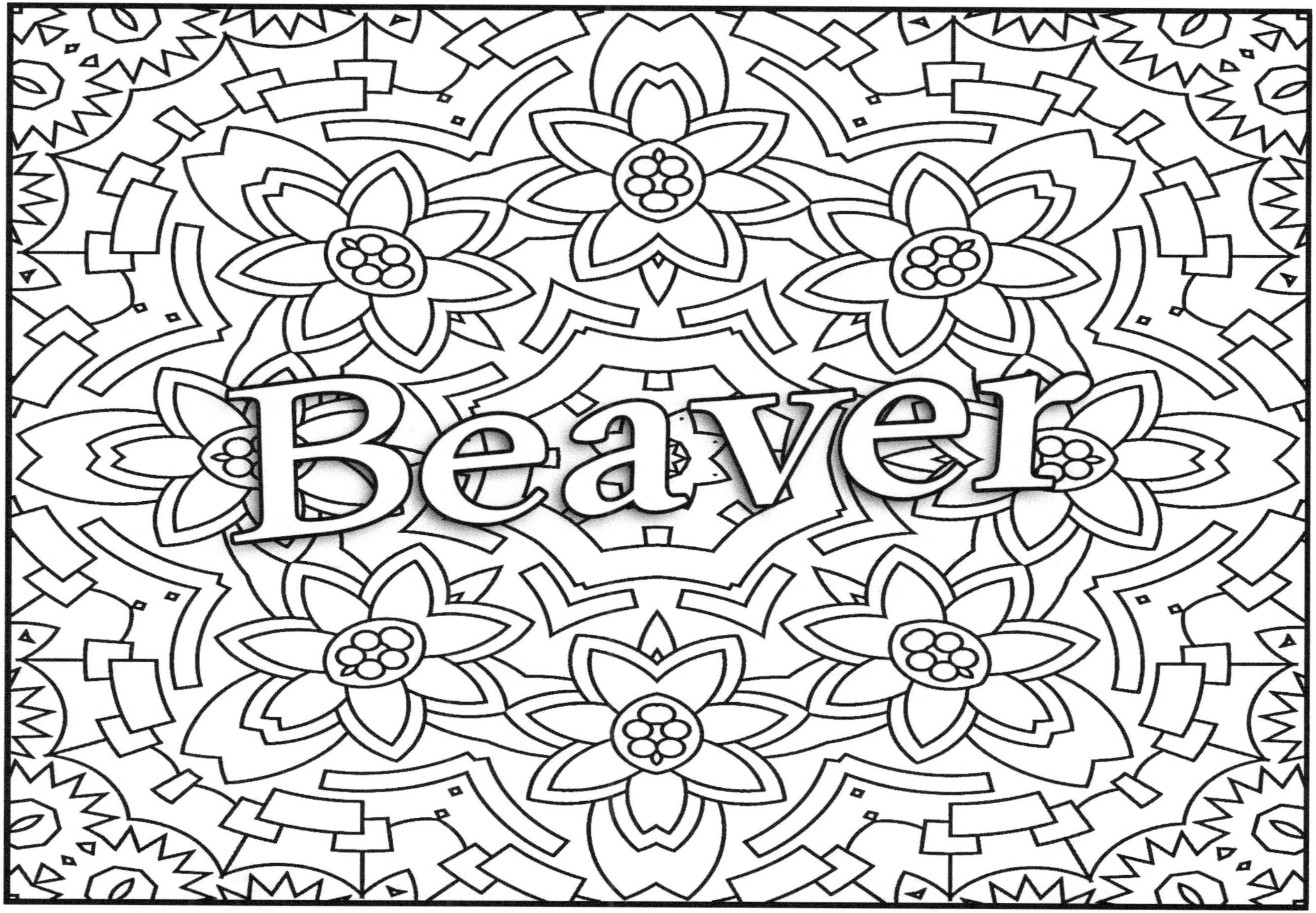
Beaver

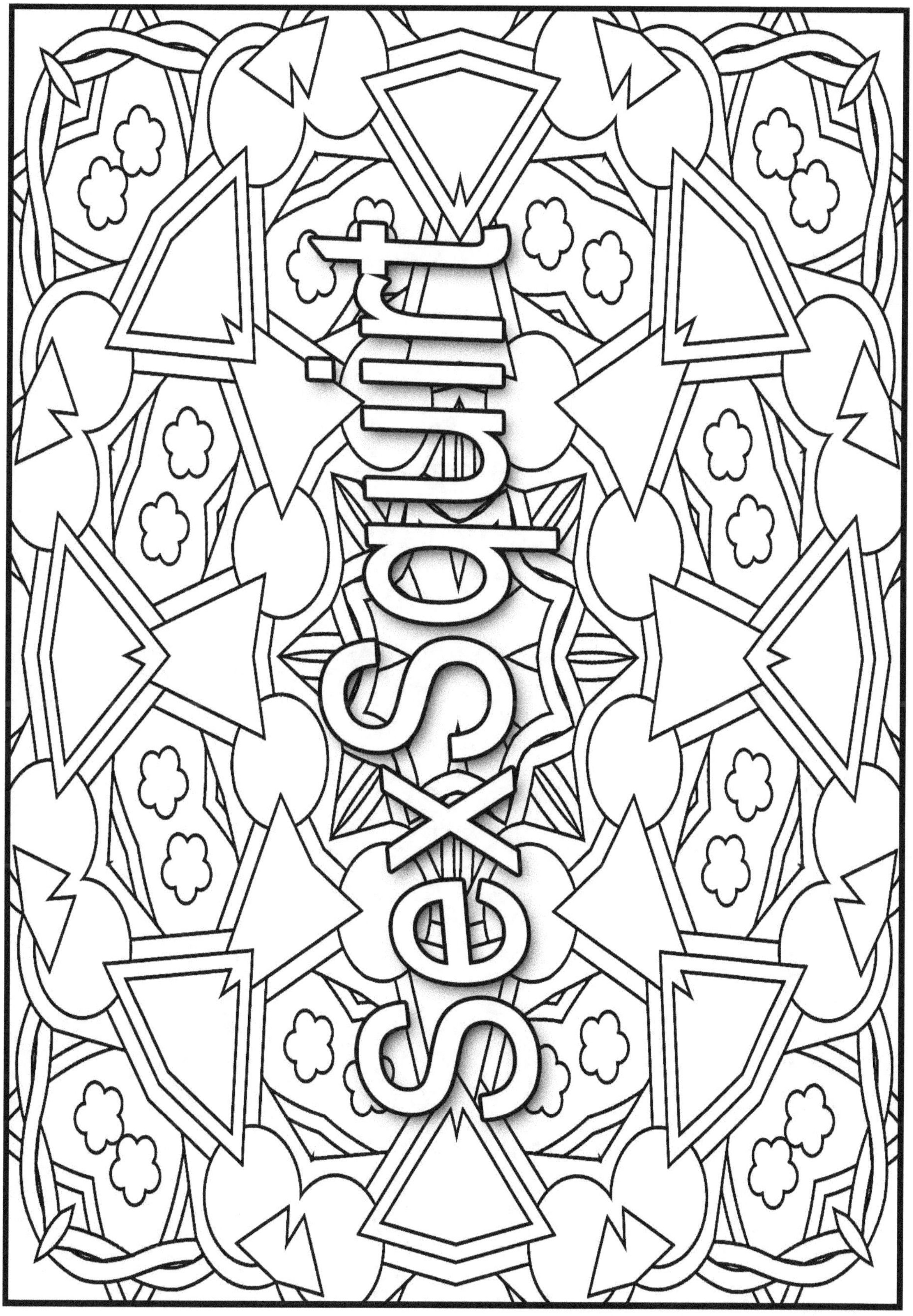
SexSplurt

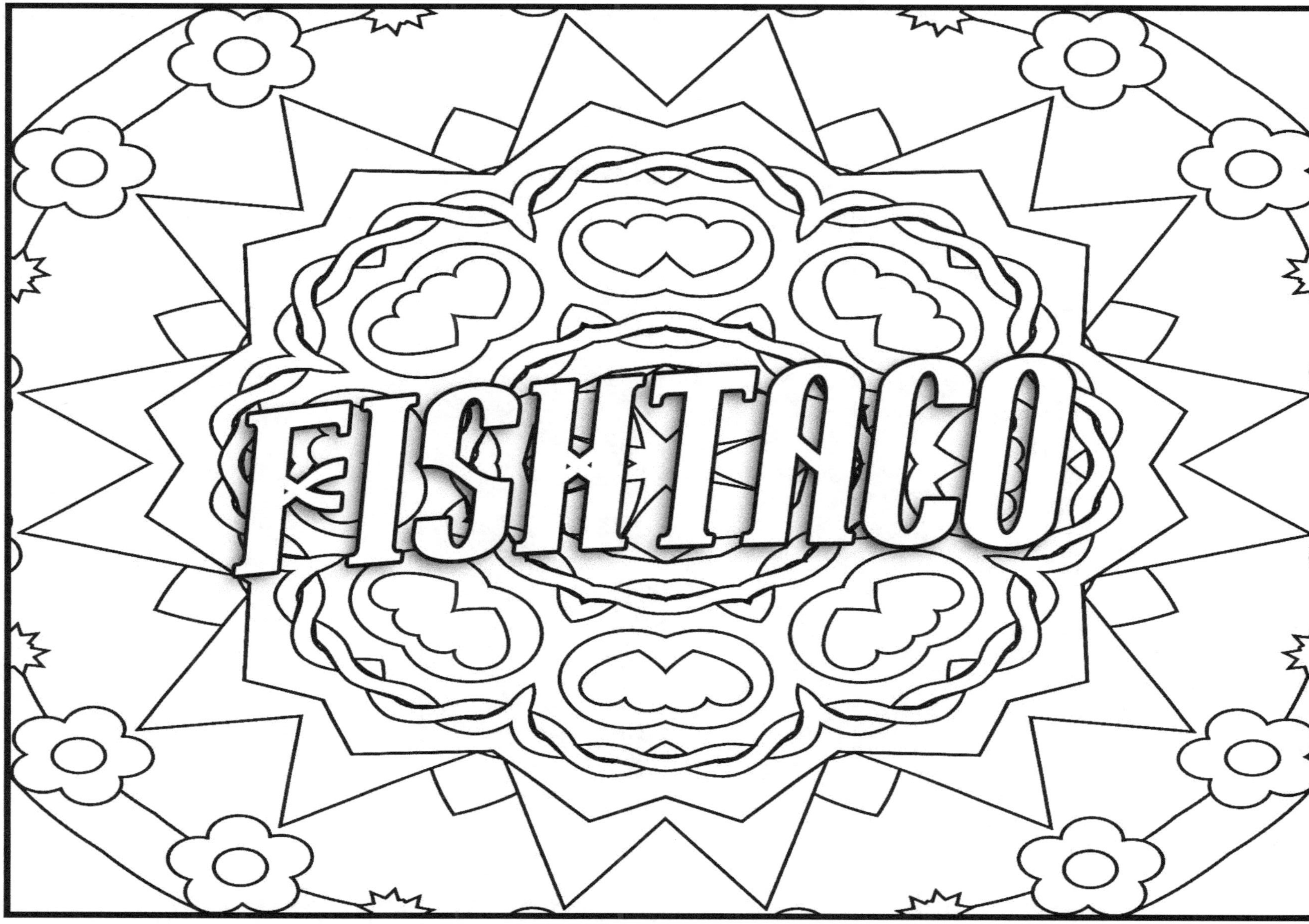
FISHTACO

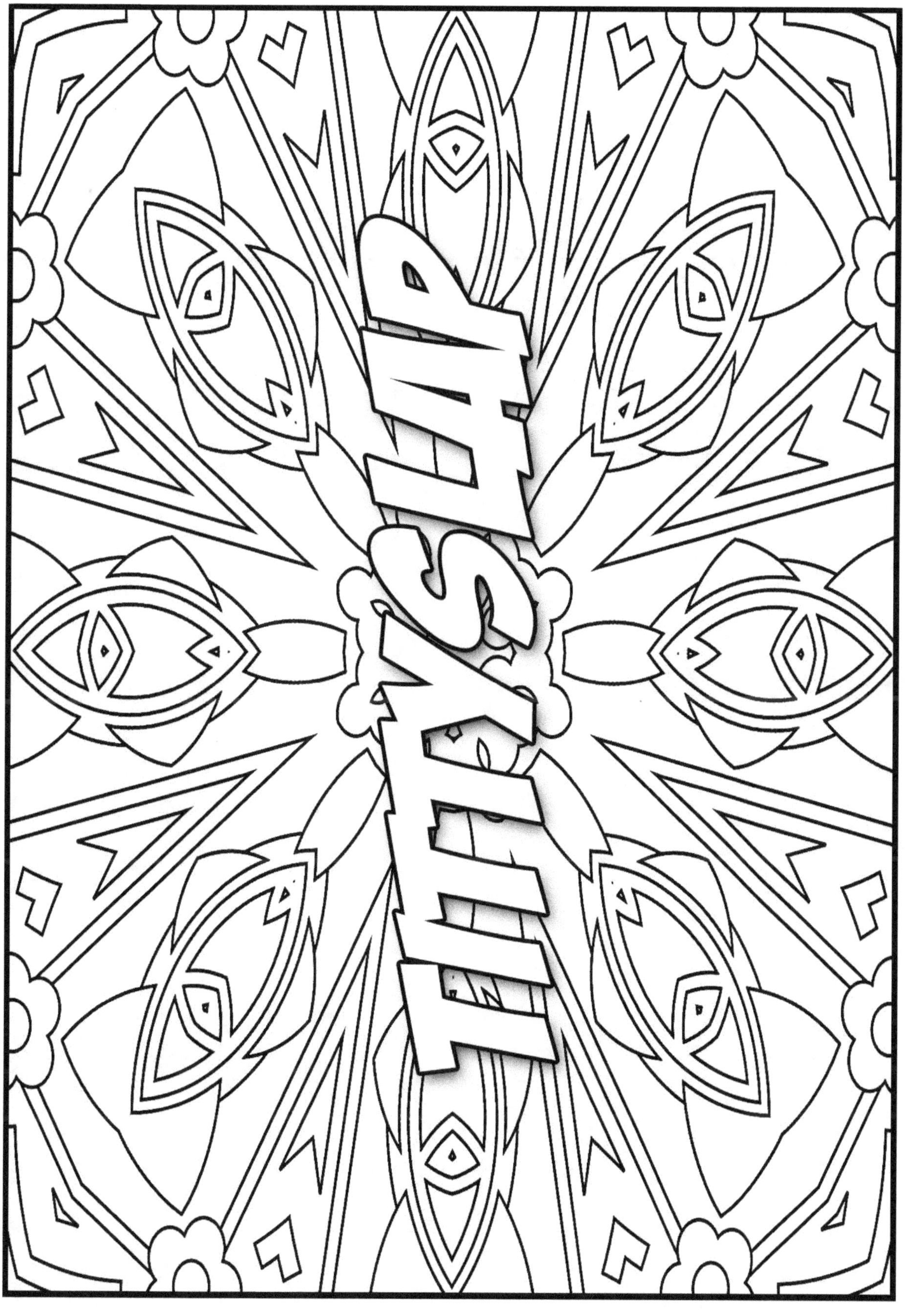
TITTYSLAP

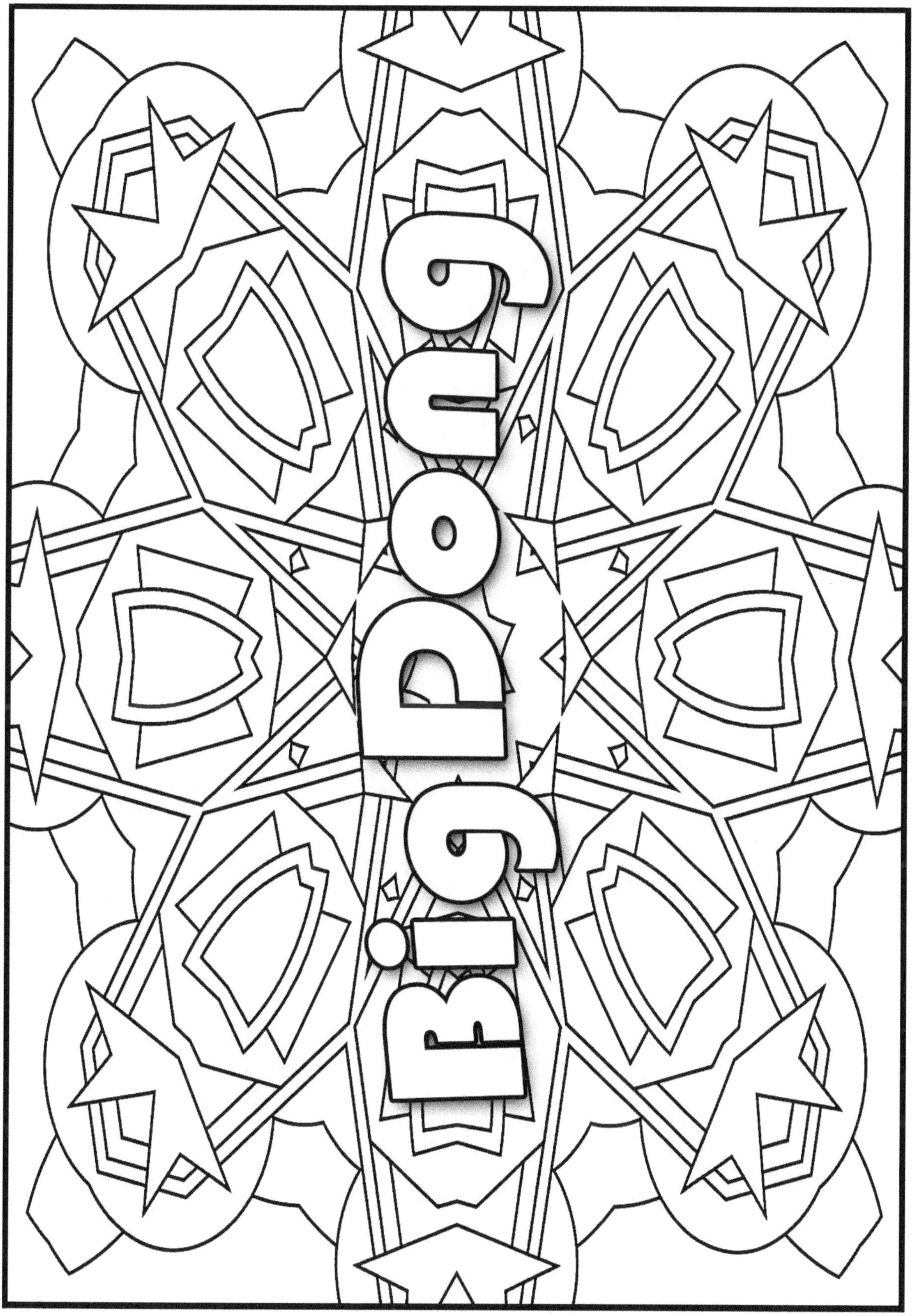
Big Dong

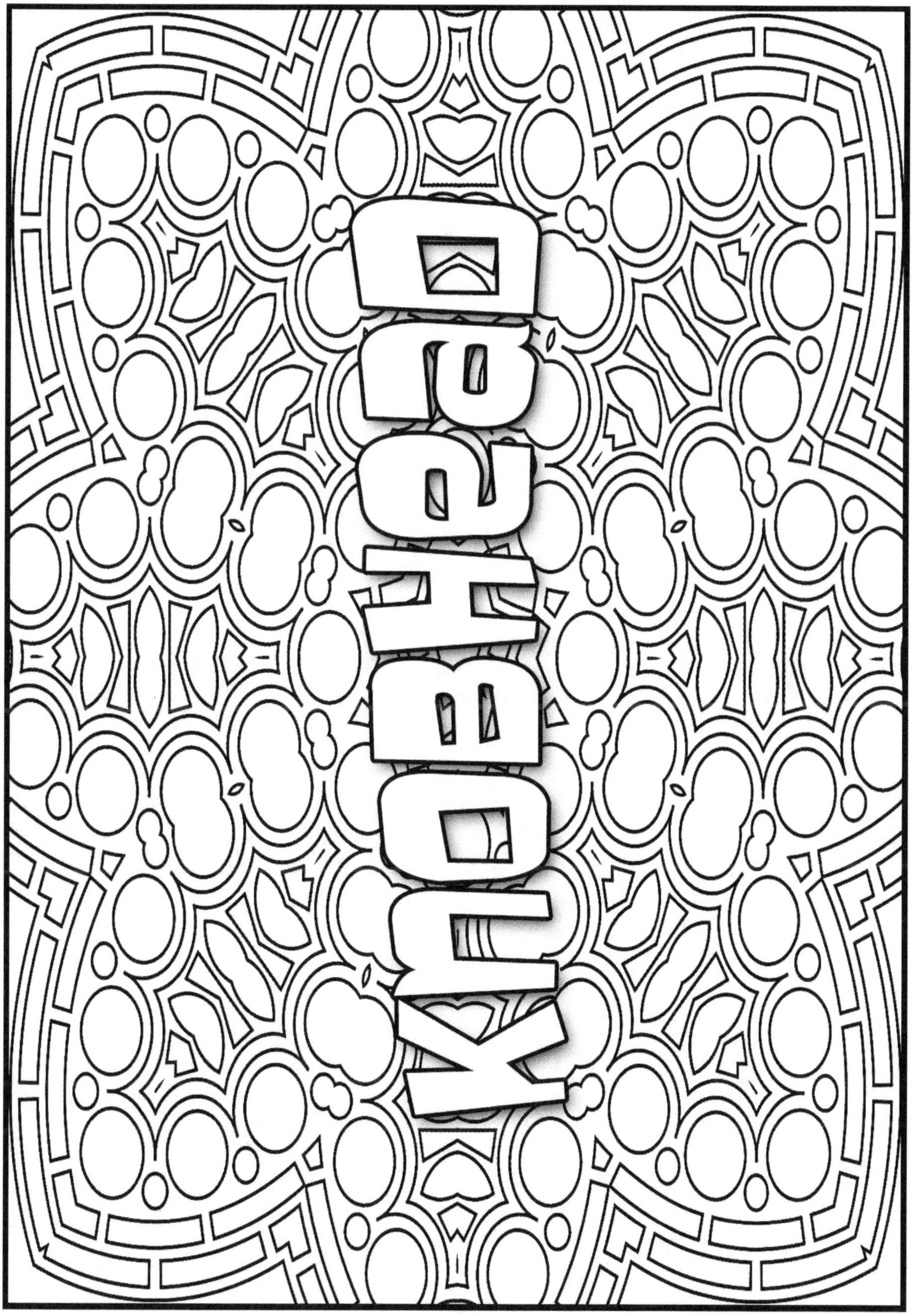
Knobhead

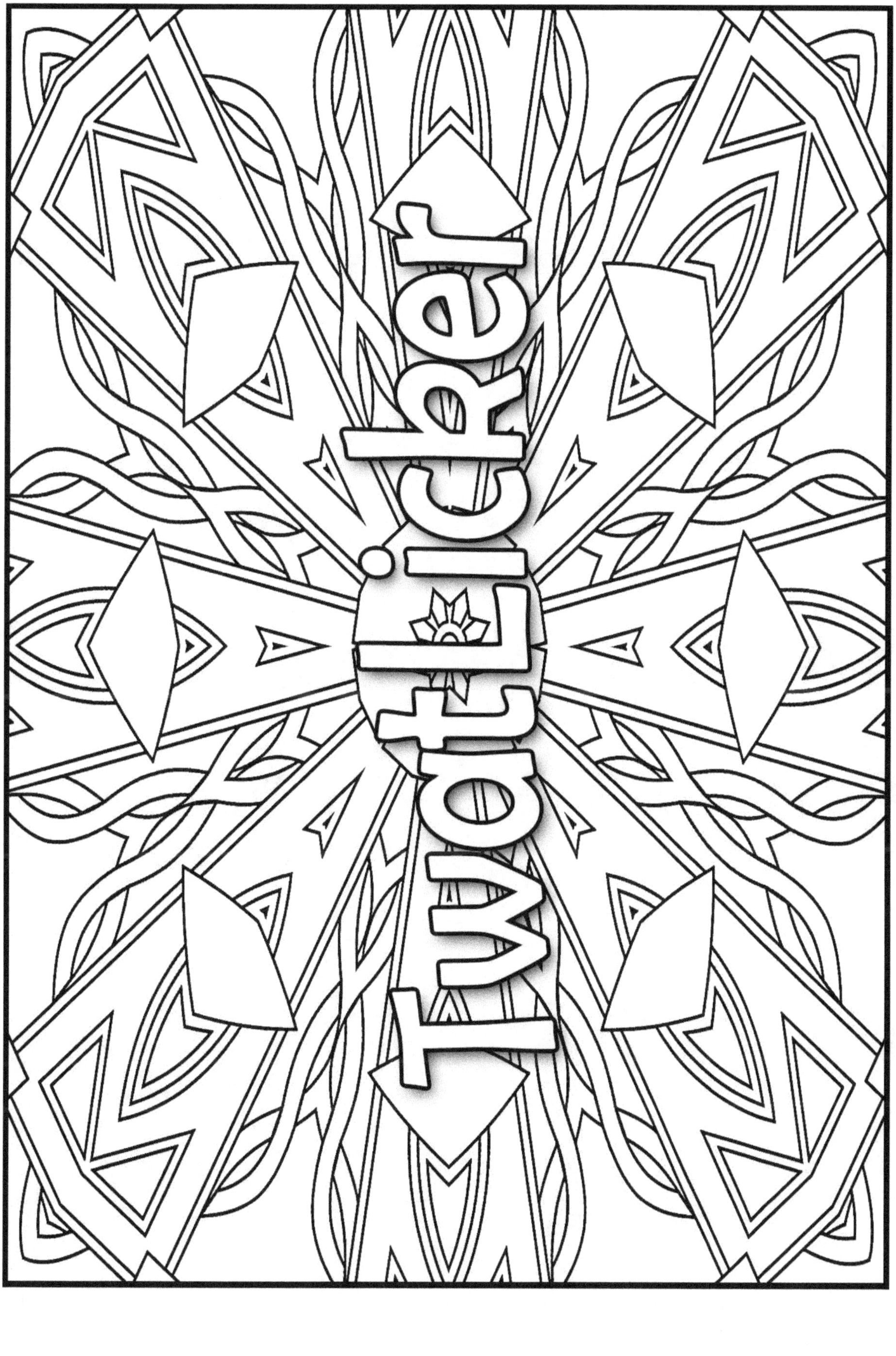
Twatlicker

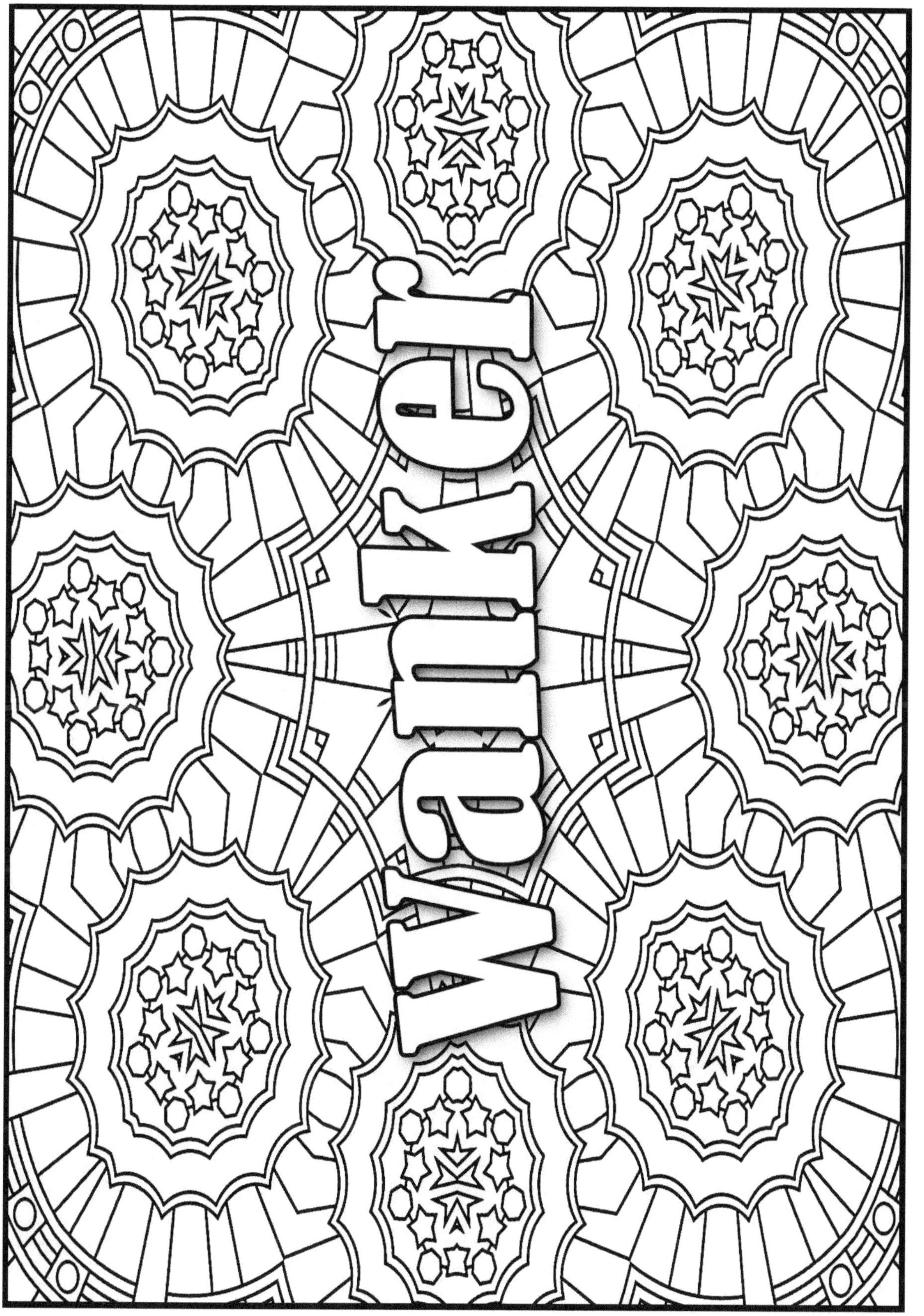
wanker

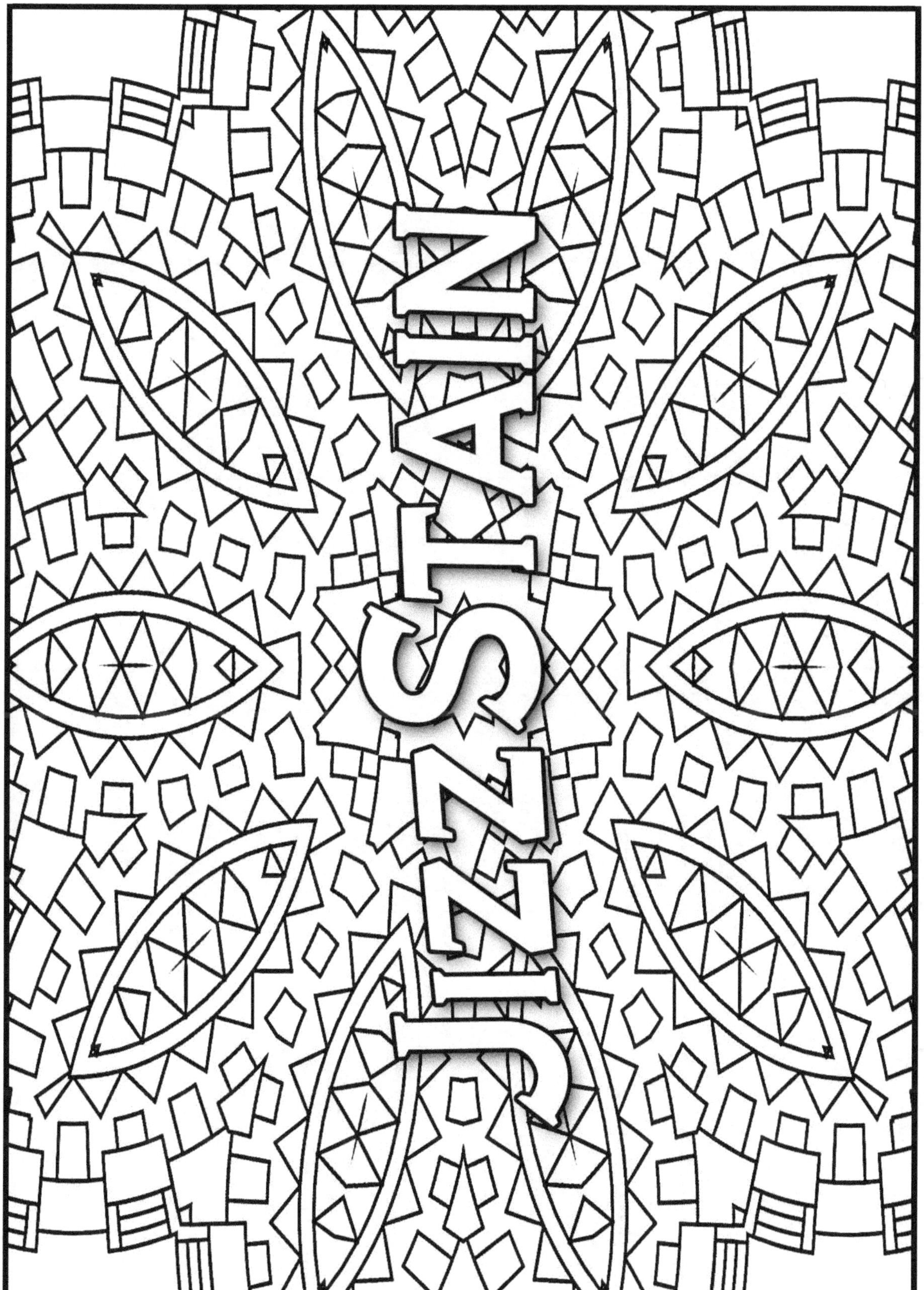
JIZZ STAIN

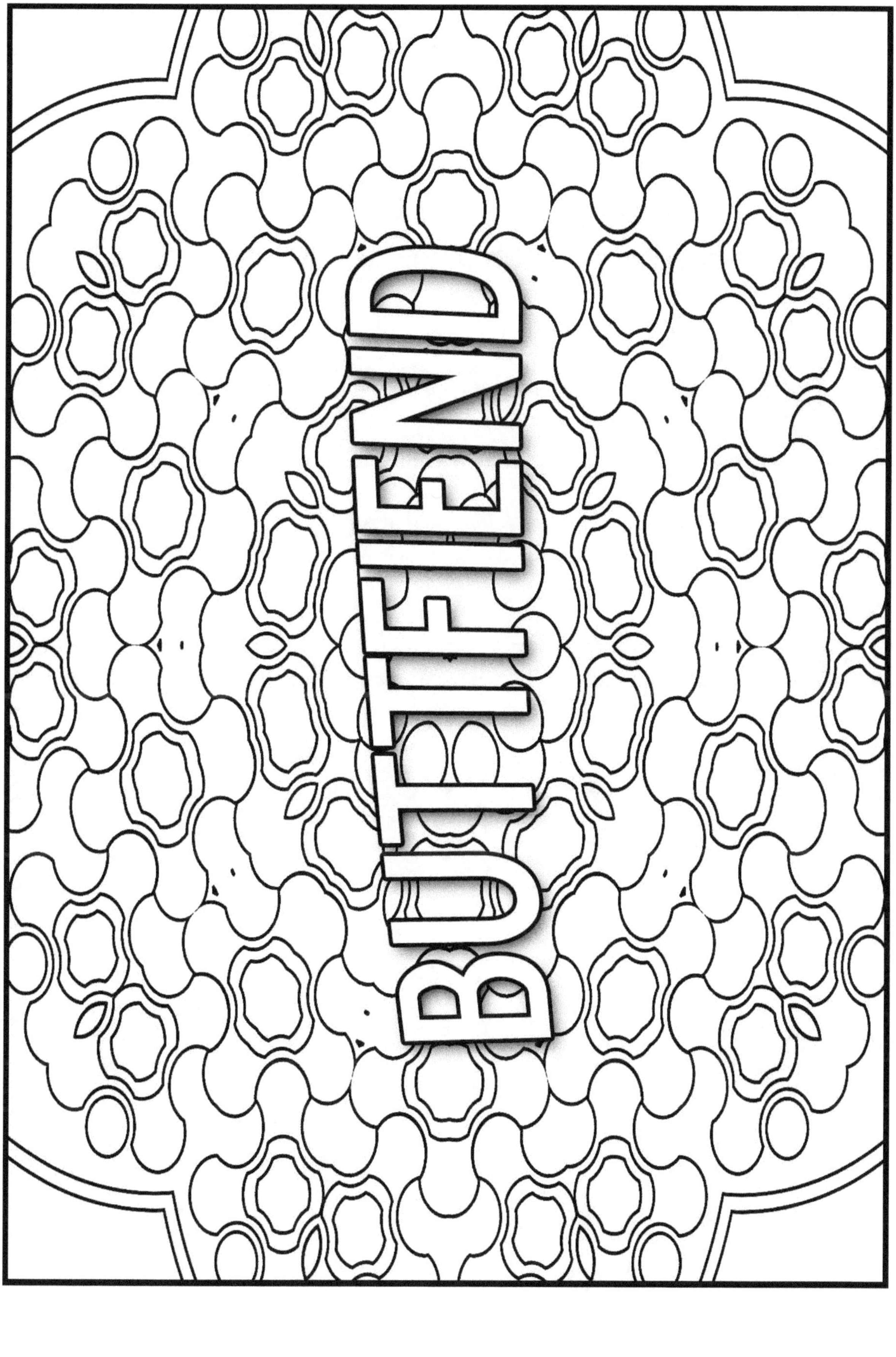
BUTTFIEND

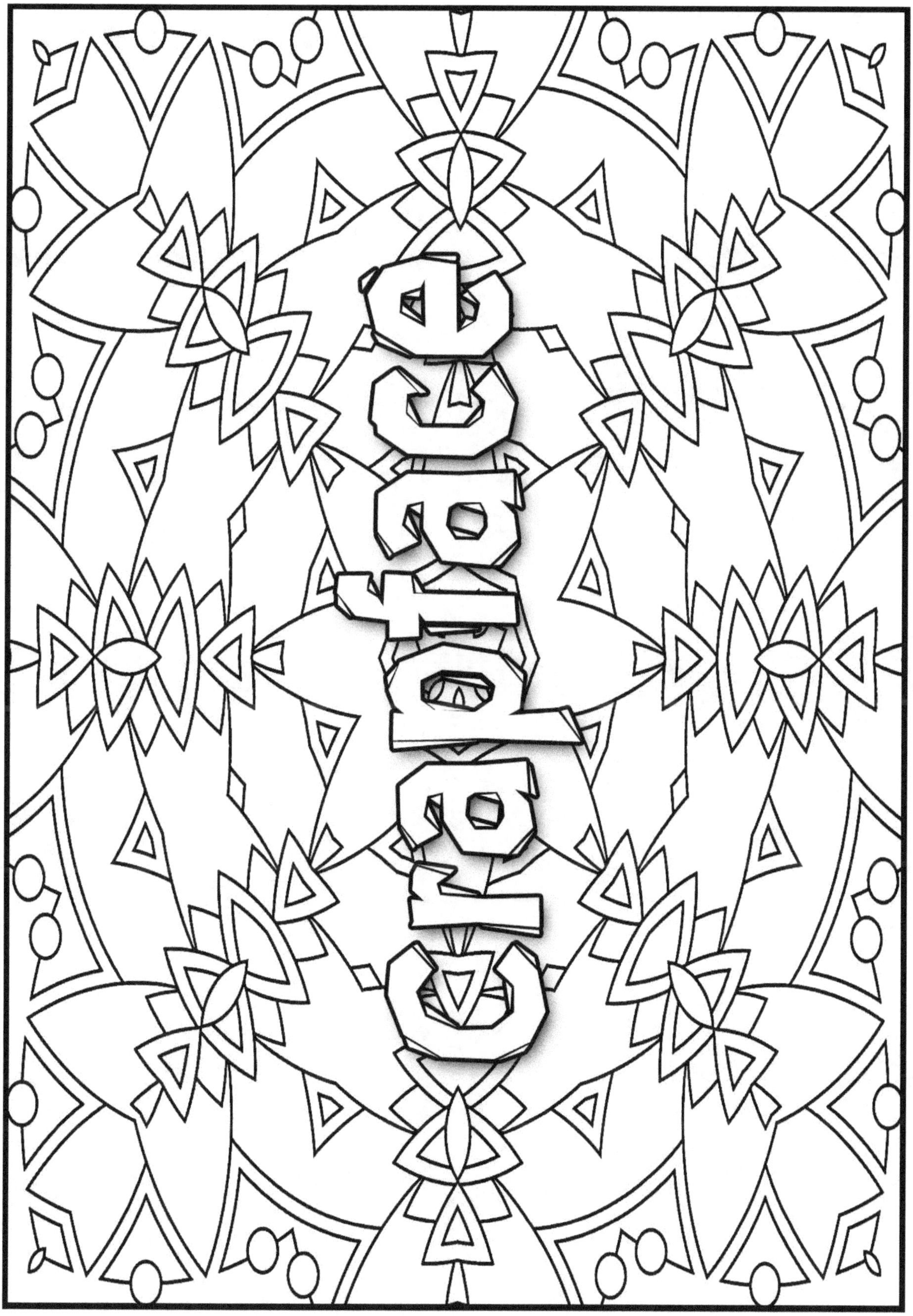
crapface

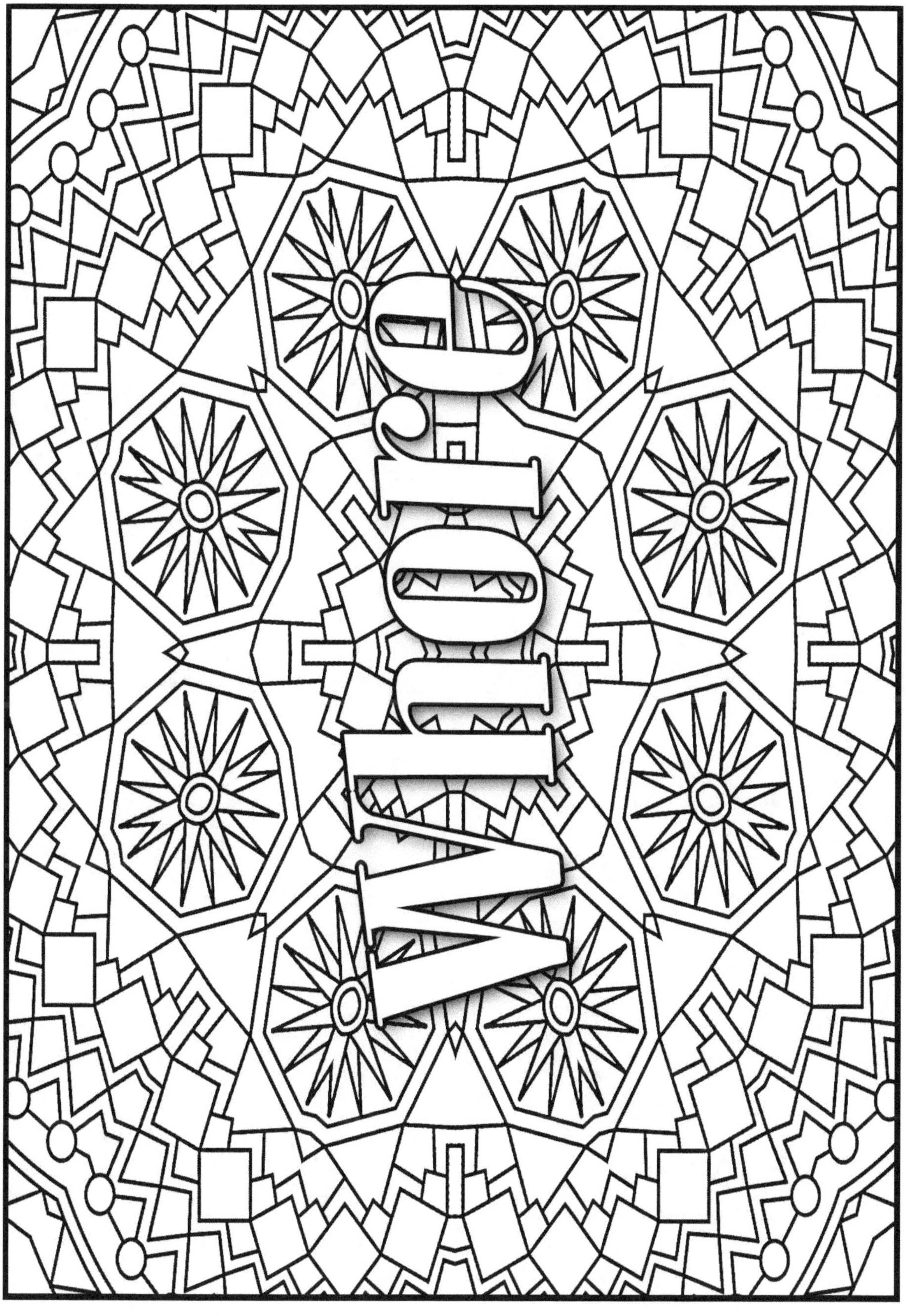
Whore

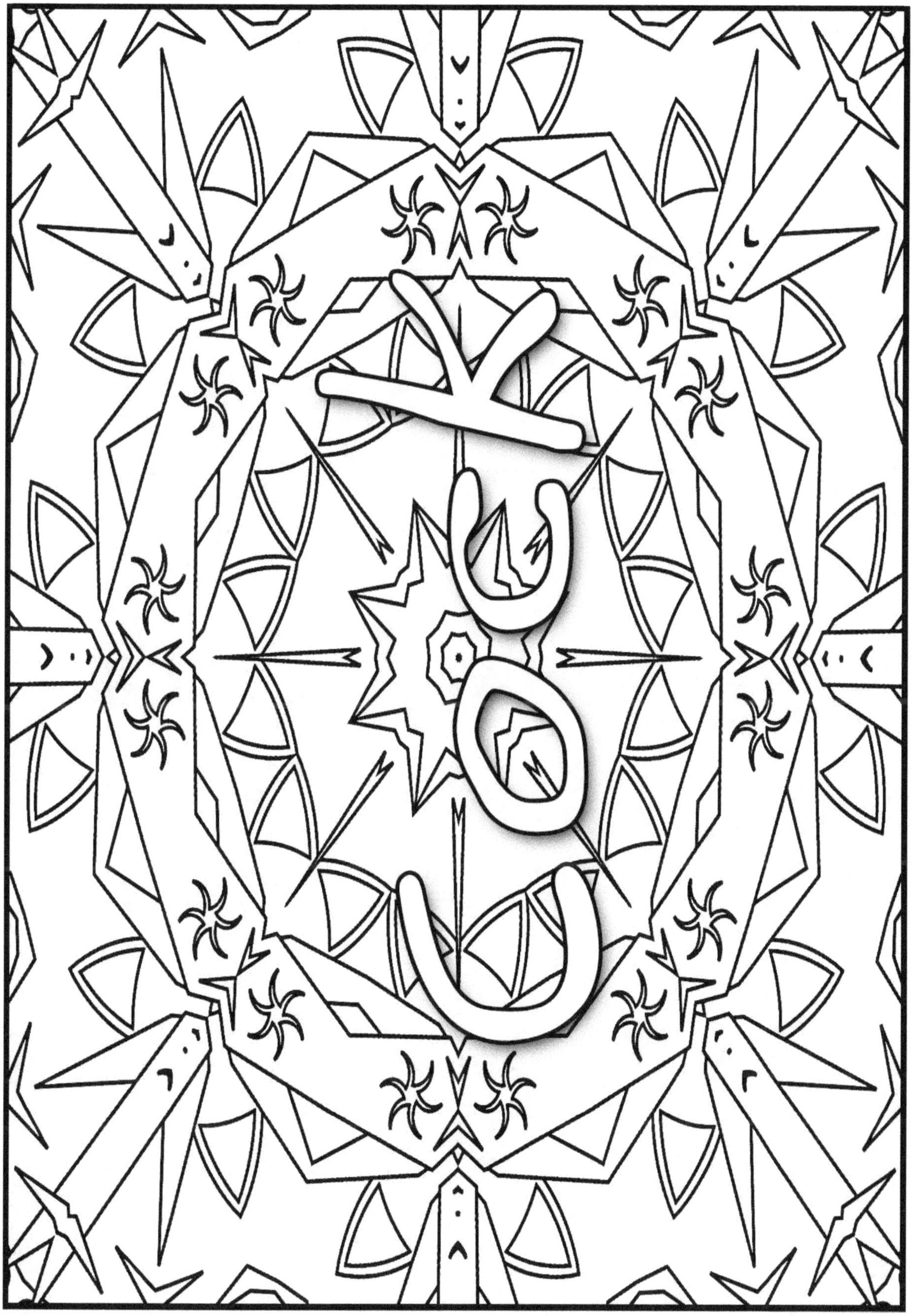
Cock

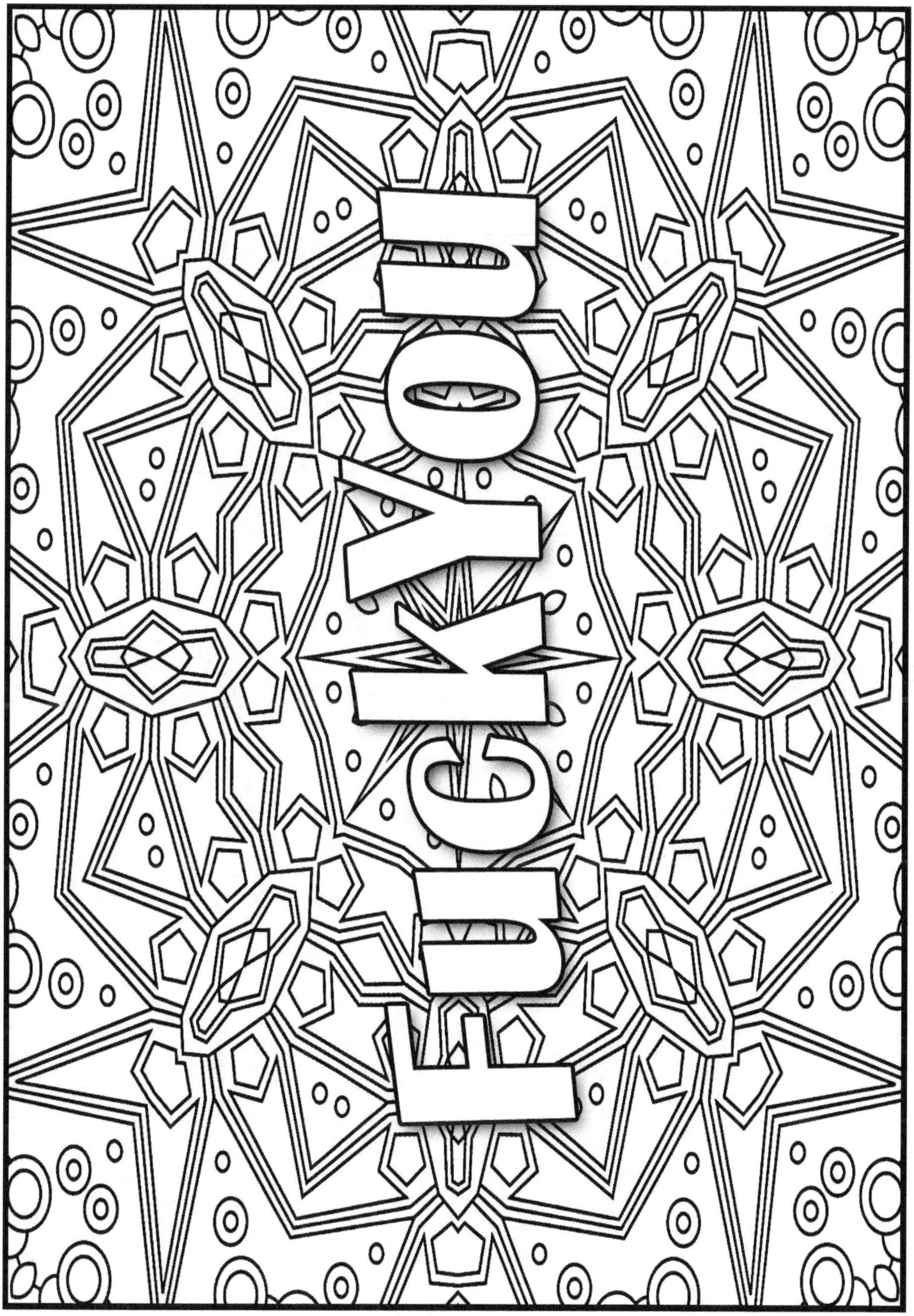
Fuck You